OUR EVANGELICAL FAITH

OUR EVANGELICAL FAITH

By

HAROLD JOHN OCKENGA

Pastor, Park Street Congregational Church,
Boston, Mass.

Author, *Have You Met These Women?*,
Our Protestant Heritage, etc.

Foreword by Leslie R. Marston

WIPF & STOCK · Eugene, Oregon

Wipf and Stock Publishers
199 W 8th Ave, Suite 3
Eugene, OR 97401

Our Evangelical Faith
By Ockenga, Harold John and Rosell, Garth M.
Copyright©1946 by Ockenga, Harold John
ISBN 13: 978-1-5326-7412-9
Publication date 10/26/2018
Previously published by Zondervan, 1946

PREFACE

The Statement of Faith of the National Association of Evangelicals was forged from the collective convictions of evangelical leaders from many denominations assembled at St. Louis in April, 1942. It was unanimously adopted at the Constitutional Convention of the National Association of Evangelicals at Chicago in 1943. The statement represents the Christian faith held in common by evangelical Christians ranging from high Calvinists to Pentecostals. It does not embody the entire system of doctrine held by any denominational group in constituent membership in the National Association of Evangelicals. Each body has doctrines beyond this common precious faith. The movement emphasizes the agreements—not the differences—of its members.

Since these truths are affirmed by all, I felt it incumbent upon me to interpret them to my people. Conse quently, this series was preached in the Park Street Church at the evening services, which are broadcast to all New England. They were well received. Dr. Murch, editor of *United Evangelical Action*, requested me to print them in that publication. These messages are being published for wider distribution in response to the demands of enthusiastic readers.

My own theological views are presented in these discourses which are not to be construed as the official interpretations of the National Association of Evangelicals.

HAROLD JOHN OCKENGA.
Boston, Mass.

NATIONAL ASSOCIATION OF EVANGELICALS

Statement of Faith

1. We believe the Bible to be the inspired, the only infallible, authoritative word of God.

2. We believe that there is one God, eternally existent in three persons: Father, Son and Holy Spirit.

3. We believe in the deity of our Lord Jesus Christ, in His virgin birth, in His sinless life, in His miracles, in His vicarious and atoning death through His shed blood, in His bodily resurrection, in His ascension to the right hand of the Father, and in His personal return to power and glory.

4. We believe that for the salvation of lost and sinful man, regeneration by the Holy Spirit is absolutely essential.

5. We believe in the present ministry of the Holy Spirit by whose indwelling the Christian is enabled to live a godly life.

6. We believe in the resurrection of both the saved and the lost; they that are saved unto the resurrection of life and they that are lost unto the resurrection of damnation.

7. We believe in the spiritual unity of believers in Christ.

FOREWORD

There was a need for this book and Dr. Ockenga was best qualified to write it.

The author's public utterances and written words always command deep respect for the scholarship they reflect, the integrity and sincere conviction that fill his words, and his clear definition of the essentials of conservative belief.

It is especially fitting that Dr. Ockenga permit the publication of these discourses which give his elaboration of the doctrinal witness of the National Association of Evangelicals. He was a leader in organizing evangelical forces, was the Association's first president, and has been recognized as the movement's intellectual and doctrinal interpreter.

The author of this book has skillfully drawn upon his wide experience with evangelical groups and his thorough knowledge of Christian doctrine and history to set forth the heart-center of evangelical belief.

This book is no drab residium of dogma reached by cancellation of all doctrinal variations among evangelicals, for Dr. Ockenga has poured into these pages his own emphatic personality and has high-lighted them from his own doctrinal angle. Fellow Calvinists may feel that the author's Calvinism is too moderate at some points, and at other points Arminians of the Wesleyan tradition will question the implications of his Calvinistic slant. But *Our Evangelical Faith* will serve to define for evangelicals their agreement in essentials and the frontiers beyond which each group has developed its distinctive pattern.

We predict that this book will clarify doctrinal preaching in many pulpits and will guide the study of conservative groups which seek a clear understanding of the common heritage of evangelical Christianity and the relationship of their respective emphases.

LESLIE R. MARSTON,
Past President, National
Association of Evangelicals.

CONTENTS

CHAPTER I

THE FINGER OF GOD

And He gave unto Moses, when he had made an end of communing with him on Mount Sinai, two tables of testimony, tables of stone, written with the finger of God (Exodus 31:18).

The finger of God is a figure for the inspired Word of God. It is a phrase which represents the power of God, the direct action of His own immediate energy.

The magicians of Egypt recognized this energy of God working in the plagues and they announced in reference to the plague of lice, "This is the finger of God." Similarly, when the Lord Jesus Christ exorcised demons, men questioned the power by which He accomplished this, and accused Him of doing it through the power of Beelzebub, the prince of devils. In answer, He said, "But if I with the finger of God cast out devils, no doubt the kingdom of God is come upon you" (Luke 11:20). Matthew 12:28 records the same incident by saying, "But if I cast out devils by the Spirit of God, then the kingdom of God is come unto you." Hence we conclude in the equation of these two, the finger of God and the Spirit of God, that the activity of the finger of God is the activity of the Spirit of God. This affords an adequate explanation of a troublesome and current problem regarding the law and it gives an illustration of the principle of inspiration which is applicable to all the Scriptures.

The law was given through Moses in three stages. First, there was the oral stage recorded in the nineteenth and twentieth chapters of the book of Exodus. We read, "Moses went up unto God, and the Lord called unto him out of the mountain, saying . . ." Also, "And Moses returned the words of the people unto the Lord." And, "God spake all these words, saying I am the Lord thy God . . ." Moses brought this law back to the people, standing at the base of the mountain, who had heard the thunderings, seen the lightnings, heard the noise of the trumpet, and witnessed the mountain smoking. They said unto Moses, "Speak thou with us, and we will hear: but let not God speak with us, lest we die." This was the first stage in the giving of the law.

The second stage was a work of God; He wrote the law upon tablets of stone. Exodus 31:18 says, "And He gave unto Moses, when He had made an end of communing with him on Mount Sinai, two tables of testimony, tables of stone, written with the finger of God." When the sinful Israelites interrupted the communing of God and Moses by worshiping the golden calf, Moses came down from the mountain with the two tables of testimony in his hand. The Scripture says, "And the tables were the work of God, and the writing was the writing of God, graven upon the tables . . . and it came to pass, as soon as he came nigh unto the camp, that he saw the calf, and the dancing: and Moses' anger waxed hot, and he cast the tables out of his hands, and brake them beneath the mount." This was the second stage of the giving of the law. Moses destroyed this record by breaking it in pieces.

The third stage is initiated by the Lord's order to Moses following his effective intercession in behalf of the people. God said, "Hew thee two tables of stone like unto the first: and I will write upon these tables the words that were in the first tables, which thou breakest." Then the Scripture hastily adds in the twenty-eighth verse of the thirty-fourth chapter, "And he (Moses) was there with the Lord forty days and forty nights: he did neither eat bread, nor drink water. And he wrote upon the tables the words of the covenant, the ten commandments. And it came to pass,

when Moses came down from Mount Sinai with the two
tables of testimony in Moses' hand, when he came down
from the mount that Moses wist not that the skin of his
face shone while he talked with him." Here we are told
that Moses wrote the tables of the law and yet they are
called the writing of the Lord. Moreover when Moses
summarized this in his speech in Deuteronomy 10:1-4, he
referred to it in the following words, "The Lord said unto
me, hew thee two tables of stone like unto the first, and
come up unto me into the mount, and make thee an ark
of wood. And I will write on the tables the words that
were in the first tables which thou breakest, and thou
shalt put them in the ark." It is very clear that what
Moses wrote is called the writing of the Lord. Obviously
God has no finger, for that is anthropomorphic language,
but he exercised his power through Moses to whom he
communicated his law "face to face."

This leads us to see that God spake to Moses so that he
received a revelation; that Moses wrote so that his writing
was God's writing; and that this infallible revelation is
authoritative—God's Word. On a larger scale, that is the
story of the whole Bible.

The inspiration of the Bible as the work of God written by the finger of God is the dividing watershed of all
Christian thinking. The modern mind is afraid of the
charge of literalism. This fear has led to all kinds of erron-
eous thought and speculation concerning the Bible. Some
of our most prominent modern writers reason toward
Biblical conceptions without the Biblical authority. They
do not want to quote the Bible lest the stigma of literalism
be placed upon them. Can we still believe in the doctrine
of an authoritative book? The National Association says,
"We believe the Bible to be the inspired, the only infallible,
authoritative word of God."

I. REVELATION — GOD SPOKE

The fact of revelation is clearly stated in the Bible. Hebrews 1:1 says, "God, who at sundry times and in divers manners spake in times past unto the fathers by the prophets, hath in these last days spoken unto us by his Son." The important thing is that God has spoken. An objective series of events stands behind the record called God's revelation. God did something in the creation, in the flood, in the deliverance of the Israelites from Egypt, in the care of the Israelites during the wilderness and their entrance into Canaan land. God did something on Mount Sinai. These may be called the redemptive deeds of God and they culminated in the atonement of Calvary and the giving of the Holy Spirit. Those redemptive deeds of revelation are not yet completed, for Christ is yet to be revealed from heaven, and will take vengeance on those who know not God. That is a redemptive act and constitutes a revelation of God.

God supplemented these redemptive deeds by conversation with Abraham, Moses, Samuel, and others of His chosen prophets whereby they came to know Him. An interpretation of these redemptive deeds was given in the prophetic word through holy men of God under the influence of the Holy Spirit. How that revelation was given will be discussed later, but the revelation itself originated in God and made itself known unto receptive men. Either this is true or men such as Moses, Samuel, David and Ezra exploited their imaginations in passing off myths and fables as revealed from God. The moral tone of the Bible forbids that as it commends itself to our own conscience.

The possibility of such a revelation depends upon our theistic belief, namely our belief in a God who created, governs and controls the universe. The acceptance or rejection of that is arbitrary, but it is simple to see that he who rejects theism can have no place for revelation and must explain it away. His predisposition would be against revelation.

The form of revelation is as essential as the fact of revelation. Revelation is a communication of supernatural knowledge from God, His purposes, the secrets of grace, the future of His church in the world and the life of the soul after death. There is no way of learning about these things except through God's revelation. Hence, the Bible assumes that conversation between God and man is possible. God spoke to Moses with a voice out of the cloud. He spoke with Samuel and he spoke with the Lord Jesus Christ and he spoke with Paul. This conversation is no doubt the highest form of revelation.

Another form of corresponding revelation, however, came in the appearances of God before the incarnation. God appeared to Abraham in the Plain of Mamre, to Lot in the city of Sodom, to Joshua before the gates of Jericho; to Gideon by the threshing floor. These we hold to be the temporary appearances of the Second Person of the trinity in human form before the incarnation, called epiphanies. Through them revelations were made unto men. There is also the form of vision. Elisha had his vision of the chariot of fire. Daniel had visions. The vision of the handwriting on the wall at Belshazzar's palace was given to many. In these ways God revealed himself.

Another form is dreams. Jacob dreamed of the ladder going from Bethel to heaven. Joseph dreamed concerning himself, concerning the future of the butler and the baker, concerning the famines in Egypt. Nebuchadnezzar dreamed of the times of the Gentiles and his dream was interpreted by Daniel. Even heathen, such as Abimelech, learned the will of God through dreams. Still another form is the direct mental suggestions made unto individuals whose capacities were heightened by the Holy Spirit. The forms of revelation are numerous.

The finality of revelation rests in Jesus Christ. In Him God Himself became flesh and dwelt among us. He was seen, handled, looked upon and heard. He exegeted the Father and he made God known unto men. Therefore his words, deeds and life were the words, deeds, and life of God. The teaching of Christ filled and completed the older parts of revelation. He said, "Think not that I am come to destroy the law, or the prophets, I am not come to destroy, but to fulfill." Nevertheless, these deeds of God in Christ had to be interpreted. So He remained for forty days after His resurrection to instruct His disciples in the things pertaining to the kingdom of God, namely, the meaning of His death, His burial, His resurrection, the nature of His church and the work which they were to do. He communicated unto them the truth which they as the authoritative spokesmen of Christianity were to propagate.

II. Inspiration — Moses Wrote So That His Writing Was God's Writing

That is the meaning of inspiration. Inspiration does not refer to revelation, but to the recording of revelation. In its original sense, it certainly applies unto the receiver of revelation who was an inspired man, but in its accepted sense it refers to the individual who wrote the revelation under the inspiration of the Holy Ghost. Inspiration, according to the Bible, is the influence of the Holy Spirit upon the minds of the writers of the Bible so that they correctly recorded the revelation of God's mind and will.

This does not assume that everything in the Bible was received from revelation, but that everything taught in the Bible is true. The historical writers such as Ezra and

Luke may have had no revelation, but they were rendered infallible teachers by inspiration. Moses may have received much of his information from tradition taught to him by his mother in the Nile Valley, and yet the activity of the Holy Spirit enabled him to teach the truth.

God set these holy men, selected providentially and prepared over the years for this purpose, apart as "inspired," so that they were qualitatively distinct from other believers of the Old and New Testament who were merely illuminated by the Holy Spirit. According to Paul the Holy Spirit has diversities of gifts. Some men became the organs of God so that what they taught, God taught.

The method of inspiration has always been a matter of controversy. "Mechanical dictation" is the one method to which most objections have arisen. This comes from the fact that men think mechanical dictation means God dictated to men who passively received his dictation as amanuenses. I am sure that if God did the dictating, I would be very glad to receive the dictation and I would have no objection to that theory, but the Bible does not teach this. Nothing, in fact, is farther from the truth, for the various writers of the Bible used their different vocabularies, gifts, methods of thought and logical processes. These forty different writers can easily be distinguished as farmers, shepherds, priests and musicians. If God had dictated this mechanically, the words of the Bible, the vocabulary, would have been the same throughout. Furthermore, verbal inspiration often is confused with dictation. However, unless a clear distinction is made, verbal inspiration implies only one vocabulary, one style, one form in the Bible, and that is not true. Verbal inspiration, therefore, must mean something else.

Men were the intelligent, voluntary, cooperative agents of God, and were so affected by the Holy Ghost that in their thinking, willing and living they became the organs of God. Their human faculties were not suspended, but heightened and elevated. Hence, the various parts of the Bible are extremely different one from another.

"Moved upon" actually described the elevation and superintendence of the Holy Ghost, so that in writing they were preserved from error and they infallibly taught what God intended should be taught. This is the doctrine of the Bible. Jesus said, "But the comforter, which is the Holy Ghost, whom the Father will send in my name, He shall teach you all things, and bring all things to your remembrance, whatsoever I have said unto you." Paul said, "We speak the wisdom of God in a mystery, even the hidden wisdom, which God ordained before the world unto our glory: Which none of the princes of this world knew: for had they known it, they would not have crucified the Lord of glory . . . But God hath revealed them unto us by his Spirit: for the Spirit searcheth all things, yea, the deep things of God." He also said to the Thessalonians, "When ye received the word of God which ye heard of us, ye received it not as the word of men, but as it is in truth, the word of God, which effectually worketh also in you that believe." He wrote to Timothy, "All Scripture is given by inspiration of God, and is profitable for doctrine, for reproof, for correction, for instruction in righteousness." Peter declares, "Holy men of God spake as they were moved by the Holy Ghost." And the Lord Jesus Christ said, "The Scripture cannot be broken."

The manisfestation of inspiration is found in the fact that the Bible is variously called, "The Scripture," "Scriptures," "The Word of God," which suggests that they are plenarily inspired. Christ said that David by the Spirit called Messiah Lord, in Matthew 22:43. The writer of the book of Hebrews says that David's words in Psalm 95, "Harden not your hearts . . . " are the words of the Holy Ghost (Heb. 3:7). The apostles attributed in Acts 4:25

the words of David in Psalm 2 to God saying, "Who by the mouth of thy servant David has said." Paul claimed that Isaiah's words were the words of the Holy Ghost. "Well spake the Holy Ghost by Isaiah . . . " (Acts 28.25).

The inspiration of the Bible extends not only to certain revealed truths but also to all factual portions of the Bible. There is no need for an endless search for what is true or false, myth or history, accommodation to error of the day or permanent truth. Such a search leaves us without any certainty concerning God's guidance, will, purpose and teaching for us.

The very words as originally written were chosen under inspiration. Otherwise, we never could have had the thought that God intended to convey. They were the writer's own words, but were selected by God. In this sense, we have no objection to the meaning of verbal inspiration or plenary inspiration. The view that because we lack the autographs such verbal inerrancy is useless, is not valid. Historical criticism has remarkably reconstructed those autographs so that we may be sure that today we have the teaching of the original writers. There is no question of text that exists which would change a single doctrine of the Church. Christ Himself so accepted the Scriptures when He said, "If ye call them gods, unto whom the word of God came, and the scripture cannot be broken . . ."

III. AUTHORITY — GOD'S WORD IS AUTHORITATIVE FOR MAN WHETHER HE ACCEPTS IT OR NOT

The Bible is a growing revelation. Little did David think when he wrote "All things" in the eighth Psalm that "all things" meant the whole universe as the writer of the book of Hebrews says that it does. The Bible writers knew so little of the full meaning of their own writings that

under the guidance of the Holy Spirit they searched dili-
gently to understand. (I Peter 1:10.) Little were men
able to comprehend the full meaning of Scripture in their
day, but as time goes on things which were read into the
Scripture are being cast aside as new light dawns upon
them or breaks from them. The church has often slowly
relinquished views which it read into the Scriptures, but
later saw that other views were consistent. Had God not
used the phenomenal language for physical events of the
world as the best of scientists do today, saying that the
sun rises and the sun sets, the Bible would have been cast
aside by people as error when they thought in the terms of
the Ptolemaic system of astronomy. Now we find that
the new discoveries of science do not conflict with the
Bible, for the Bible uses the language of the man on the
street. To argue against the Bible by saying that the sun
stood still and therefore the whole solar system stopped
instead of the world stopping on its axis according to the
Bible is cavil, for how else would the men of that day have
described the sun standing still or how should I say the
world stood still in order that the day should be length-
ened? They used the phenomenal language of their day.
They described it as they saw it. Today we understand
what they mean, even though we have to apply modern
terms of science. The discoveries of science are not incon-
sistent with the Bible.

The Bible is an accurate and infallible record. Wherever the Bible has been tested it stands. Archeology has
been the greatest evidence of the accuracy of historical
data in the Scripture. I have read a number of books on
archeology and I have yet to find one book which proves
that the Bible is wrong historically. Sir William Ramsey
approached his investigations of the historical accuracy of
Luke in a hostile attitude. When he finished he was a
firm believer and a great defender of the Bible's accuracy.

Geology cannot be shown to be contrary to the creative days of Genesis, though men may have held and still do hold those views contrary to geology. Moreover, there are often great claims made in the name of geology which go beyond any proven scientific data.

Anthropology is still a very open question, but God must be held to have initiated the process and to have differentiated man from all other existing creatures when He breathed into him the breath of life. That there may have been a Peking man, a Neanderthal man and other pre-historic specimens may be proved true and yet have no bearing upon the book of Genesis. We hold that God had to create man and He certainly separated man from all other kinds when He breathed into him the breath of life.

The Bible commends itself to the conscience of men as no other book does. The revelation within our own souls corresponds to the revelation without and we recognize the voice of God.

The Bible has elevated, delivered and enlightened men and women wherever it has gone. It has demonstrated that it is from God.

Hence the Bible is an authoritative guide for human life today. If you would know of God, the world, man, sin, salvation and immortality, turn to the Bible, for in it God speaks and it is His word. If you would be saved from your sins, be assured of eternal life and enjoy victory over the world; obey God's word in the Bible. If you want the church to prosper, people to be changed, God's work to go on apace, align yourself with those who acknowledge the Bible to be God's word, infallible and authoritative.

Whether you are troubled over inspiration or not, God's word and voice may be heard in the Bible. Hear it and obey.

CHAPTER II

THE NATURE OF GOD

Go ye therefore, and teach all nations, baptizing them in the name of the Father, and of the Son, and of the Holy Ghost (Matthew 28:19).

We believe that there is one God, eternally existent in three persons: Father, Son and Holy Spirit.

This is the common faith of all Christians. The Apostles' Creed declares, "I believe in God the Father Almighty . . . and in Jesus Christ his only son our Lord . . . and in the Holy Ghost." The next major universally accepted creed was the creed of Nicea and of Constantinople. This says, "I believe in one God, the Father Almighty . . . and in one Lord Jesus Christ, the only begotten son of God . . . light of light, very God of very God, begotten not made . . . and I believe in the Holy Ghost, the Lord, and giver of life, who proceedeth from the Father, who with the Father and the Son together is worshipped and glorified, who spake by the prophets." In the year 451 the Chalcedon Creed reaffirmed Trinitarian Christianity and defined the dual nature of Jesus Christ as both God in His fullness and man in his fullness. I repeat, therefore, that Trinitarian Christianity is the common faith of all Christians.

As the belief in Scripture as the Word of God differentiates "evangelical" from "liberal", so belief in the Trinity distinguishes a Christian from those who forfeit the name Christian. There are monotheists who are not Christians. Christians believe in the unique deity of Jesus Christ and in the person and deity of the Holy Spirit. Therefore the apostolic benediction declares, "The grace of the Lord Jesus Christ, and the love of God, and the communion of the Holy Ghost, be with you all."

Trinitarian Christianity is the stumbling block of the unbeliever. Natural reason fails when a rational explanation of the Trinity is undertaken. It transcends the natural powers of man, as God transcends men. If we were able to comprehend God with our minds we would cease to worship Him. Hence the folly of attempting to explain the Trinity by reason. The superrational nature of the Trinity is evidence of God's revelation in the Bible, for no man could have invented the doctrine of the Trinity. No illustration can represent the Trinity perfectly, although threeness is stamped upon everything in nature. The natural world is composed of time, space and matter, no more, no less. Time is composed of past, present and future, no more, no less. Matter is composed of substance, attributes and relationship, no more, no less. He who studies nature ought to find many suggestions of the nature of God. However, the Scripture declares that the natural man cannot comprehend the Spirit of God, for He is spiritually discerned. At these mysteries of the Trinity, of the presence of evil in the world, of the dual nature of Christ as God and man, the natural mind reels, for it is unable to apprehend them. The next step is rebellion. The natural man wants discovery to be the means of knowledge, but Christian truths, especially this truth, are received by revelation.

The natural man repudiates essential Christian truth which centers around the Trinity. He rebels. He asserts his intellectual independence and he subjects God to the forms of his own mind. He is not willing to receive the revelation.

Yet Trinitarianism is the satisfying portion of Christianity. The relationship, offices and work of the persons of the Trinity constitute the ground of a full-orbed, redemptive theology. He who denies the deity of the Holy Spirit or the deity of the Lord Jesus Christ truncates his theology and is left with a bare theism that cannot satisfy the mind or heart. Revelation is enriched by the distinction between the Father and the Son. The fact of the Trinity makes atonement meaningful because satisfaction can be made by one person to the other person. Regeneration would be a mystery if the agency of the Holy Spirit did not make it understandable. The same is true of prayer, the church, inspiration and other doctrines of the Scripture. A realization of the redemptive work of each person of the Trinity establishes the believer. Security is received from the elective purposes of God, salvation from the atoning work of Christ and sanctification from the indwelling presence of the Holy Spirit. The Christian faith is Trinitarian faith.

I. One God

God must have substance, attributes and relationships and according to the Scripture these are interconnected. Baptism is in one name, that of the Father, Son and Holy Spirit. There are three persons, but one name, for they share one nature. Therefore when we speak of the Trinity we must remember that we believe in one God.

Christianity is a dualism, and is therefore expressive of matter and of spirit, as distinguished from materialistic monism on the one hand, and spiritualistic monism on the other. Christianity declares that there is more to the world than matter and there is more to the world than spirit. The world is real and spirit is real. We live in a dualistic universe instead of a monistic universe.

Christianity believes that God is, that He exists. He has being and therefore attributes of that being can be known.

Christianity affirms that man may know God, for God breathed into him the Spirit or breath of life. By correspondence he may know God's revelation, for an infinite spirit has spoken to a finite spirit.

The attributes of Deity are infinity, eternity and permanence. When we say that God is infinite we mean that there is no limitation upon His being, wisdom, power, holiness, justice, goodness and truth. If God is unlimited or infinite in being, he is omnipresent. There is no place where God is not present every moment. Some manifestations of the presence of God are more clear than others, but God is everywhere at once. When we speak of God being infinite or without limitation in His wisdom, we refer to His omniscience. There is nothing which God does not know. The Scripture says of Christ, "He needed not that any man should testify of man: for he knew what was in man." When we speak of God's infinite power we mean the omnipotence by which He can do all things, for example, create the world, sustain it in orderly processes and ultimately bring it into judgment. He can also interfere with the laws of the world if He so desires. We have an infinite God and all Three Persons of the Godhead are infinite.

God is eternal. This is the answer to the question "Who made God?" Nobody made God. He always was, is, and will be. He is Alpha and Omega. In the concept of the eternity of God the mind finds rest in its search for an ultimate. God is that ultimate.

God also is permanent. He is unchangeable. Nothing can be added to or detracted from these attributes of God. God has neither grown nor changed His purposes nor been taken by surprise, nor has He relinquished His control of the world. God is the same yesterday, today and forever.

God sustains certain relationships. The primary relationships which are love, position and activity, exist within the Godhead itself. The Godhead is self-sufficient. Creation was not a necessity for the self-expression of Deity.

That is one of the great values of Trinitarian Deity in our thinking. God's relationships are within Himself.

Secondary relationships are without the Godhead. In these God is independent, antecedent and supramundane. The world cannot affect God, but God can affect the world. God is independent of the world, but the world is dependent upon God.

The tertiary relationships are involved in the creation of men. This assumes a voluntary self-limitation on the part of God making men free moral agents or gods like unto Himself. In John 10:35 Jesus said, "If the Scripture calleth them gods . . . " It was of this Scripture that He said, ". . . it cannot be broken. Consequently, it is obvious that God has voluntarily limited Himself in the creation of man. He became involved in this relationship in a more real sense through the incarnation. Therefore we believe that a voluntary change took place in Deity which involved taking other beings into the divine family.

The question may be raised, "How may this be harmonized with such Scripture as Heb. 13:8; Mal. 3:6; James 1:7?" We dare not sacrifice the immutability of God. That was the error manifested in the Christological controversies of 250-450 A.D. and in the Kenosis doctrine of the last two centuries. The solution of the apparent conflict between the incarnation and the immutability of God lies in the distinction of the ancient theologians between the indwelling and the outgoing works of God. In the indwelling works of Deity, the Father, Son and Spirit share equally in all aspects of Redemption from the eternal decrees to ultimate restoration of all things. In the outgoing works of Deity, the Father does not become incarnate, nor does the Son indwell the human personality. The Son has works which the Father does not have and the Spirit has works not ascribed to the Son.

There can be no doubt that in the Son's incarnation,

assumption of human nature and exaltation to the right hand of the Father, a transition and change took place in the outgoing works of God. Certainly humanity was not the experience of Deity before the incarnation and certainly the Redeemed are to share the life of Deity after Redemption is completed. This is an interesting theological problem. Thus the Scripture says, "We are heirs of God and joint heirs with Jesus Christ."

II. THREE PERSONS

The second phase of our Trinitarian creed speaks of believing in one God and Three Persons: Father, Son and Spirit.

The Father is the ultimate. He is the absolute. He is known as "God our Father." In the salutations of the epistles He is called, "The God and Father of our Lord Jesus Christ" and to Him are ascribed the plan, decree, election and purpose of the world.

This absolute God is unknown unless He is revealed by the Son. Christ said, "No man knoweth the Son, but the Father; neither knoweth any man the Father, save the Son, and he to whomsoever the Son will reveal him." He also said, "He that hath seen me hath seen the Father ... the words that I speak unto you I speak not of myself: but the Father that dwelleth in me, he doeth the works." Christ made the Father known. He "exegeted" the Father. He taught, did and said only what the Father willed, saying, "I came down from heaven, not to do mine own will, but the will of him that sent me." In praying, Jesus Christ taught us to call God 'Our Father." Such a conception would never have come to man if the Son had not revealed it to us.

God, therefore, is unapproachable unless we approach Him through the reconciliation of the Son. God loved us and gave His only begotten Son for us, but God is holy and just and cannot be approached except through His son. Jesus said, "No man cometh unto the Father but by me." God in Christ reconciled the world unto Himself; He did not impute unto them their trespasses. Therefore God gives us access to Him through Christ and Christ's death upon the cross. Praying in Christ's Name we are heard. Coming to God through Christ we have access to His throne.

The second person of the Trinity is the Son. The Son is the eternal word, the logos of God, who was God and was with God from eternity. This is the teaching of John 1:2, Proverbs 8:22 ff., Colossians 1:18-21, Philippians 2:6 ff., etc. The Son is the only begotten of the Father, full of grace and truth. Of Him the Father says, "This day have I begotten thee." The Son is subordinate only in position. He is of the same nature and He possesses similar attributes. These are the claims that He makes when He tells us that He came to do the works of the Father, that before Abraham was He existed and that He and the Father are one. The church has always taught that Christ is of the same nature as the Father and therefore is one in being.

Christ is the executor of the Trinity in the redemptive plan. The incarnation took place, so that the God-Man was true God without sin and error. Yet He was true man in representing the redeemed. He was very God of very God and also the Son of Man. He performed His miracles which demonstrate supernatural power. He went to the Cross that He might make an atonement for our sins, so that in Him there is a propitiation through faith in His blood. He became the sovereign head of a people whose representative is in glory while they are still upon earth. The Lord Jesus Christ fulfilled the redemptive plan of the Father.

The Spirit is the third person of the Trinity. He is

called The Spirit or The Ghost, but the adjective Holy is always prefixed to it. The Holy Spirit is the gift of God, promised by God and by the Lord Jesus Christ, so that He could say, "I will pray the Father and He will send you another comforter . . . it is expedient for you that I go away, for if I go not away the Comforter can not come . . . ye shall be baptized with the Holy Ghost not many days hence." The great event of Pentecost was the advent of the Holy Spirit in His high office of comforter. It was the fulfillment of the promise of the Father. The coming of the Holy Ghost was accompanied by the gift of power for the believers. "We have not received the spirit of bondage again to fear, but the spirit of love, power and of a sound mind."

The Holy Spirit is the present agent of the Trinity in the world. He is God, omnipresent according to Psalm 129, omniscient according to I Corinthians 2:11, eternal according to Hebrews 7:14, omnipotent according to Genesis 1:2 and Luke 11:20 compared with Matthew 12:28. The Holy Spirit is a person and personality and powers are attributed unto Him. The Holy Spirit speaks. He is grieved. He wills. He has all the attributes of personality and He does God's work in the world today. The work of enlightening the minds of men, of converting men to Jesus Christ, of sanctifying the believers and of preserving them unto the coming of the Lord is the work of the Holy Spirit.

The Holy Spirit is the source of all power in the Christian life. If we would know the presence and nearness of the Triune God it must be through the Holy Spirit, for He takes of the things of God and shows them to us. The Holy Spirit is the secret of all victory. The one great need of the church is the Holy Spirit.

III. Trinitarian Faith

We believe in one God, eternally existent in three persons. Do you believe it? "He that cometh to God must believe that he is." Without faith in a Trinitarian Godhead, we simply forfeit the name "Christian."

Therefore we must bow our heads in worship before the mysterious but adorable Trinity. How three persons have the same being and attributes, how the Father and Son are one, how God was in Christ reconciling the world I know not, but I bow before that revelation in acceptance and worship. That God loved, gave, suffered, died, redeemed, I know from His revelation in which He hath made known His redemptive deeds and His prophetic words. That God may be known by a loving heart where reason staggers is true and is the experience of us all. In praying for the Ephesians St. Paul said, "That ye . . . may be able . . . to know the love of Christ, which passeth knowledge." How can we know that which passeth knowledge? Such language is paradoxical and yet it is the language of experience because we do know in our hearts that which our reason cannot comprehend.

The Lord Jesus said, "Believe in God, believe also in me." A bare theism is sterile and valueless. It can not stand alone. It must progress into revelation. That revelation came in the prophets of old, in the Lord Jesus Christ and in the New Testament prophets and apostles appointed for this purpose. It culminated in Calvary and in Pentecost. There we behold the Trinity in its full work, God the Father, God the Son and God the Holy Ghost redeeming the world. A personal trust will lead one to accept what the Trinity has done for us. This trust is saving faith.

The blessing of the Triune God upon the believing soul is wonderful. It brings election unto salvation. It brings redemption from sin's penalty and power. It brings regeneration and new faith. Repentance therefore is toward God. Faith is toward the Lord Jesus Christ. The witness is a relationship toward the Holy Spirit. Salvation is of the Triune God and not of any one Person of the Trinity.

We have need of these three works on earth to correspond with the blessed Trinity in heaven. St. John said, "There are three that bear witness in earth, the Spirit, the water, and the blood: and these three agree in one." Have you exercised repentance toward God, faith in the blood of the Lord Jesus Christ and do you possess the witness of the Spirit that you are a child of God? All these are necessary to your Christian salvation. Your Christian experience is not complete until the Holy Spirit has done His work in you. Yes, we believe in one God, eternally existent in three Persons, Father, Son and Holy Spirit.

CHAPTER III

THE CHRIST OF GOD

Believe on the Lord Jesus Christ, and thou shalt be saved (Acts 16:31).

The deity of the Lord Jesus Christ is the object of this discourse. The deity of Christ describes His nature as being the same substance with God, "God of very God," uncreated, underived, coequal with God, coeternal, immeasurable and worthy of worship. The divine being of Christ is circumscribed by the doctrine of the Trinity, namely, one God in three persons, having the same being, attributes and relationship. It was this unity of being to which Christ referred when He said, "I am in the Father and the Father in me." Again, "He that hath seen me hath seen the Father." Again, "I and my Father are one." The declaration of the same essence or oneness of being or consubstantiality of the Son of God with God is basic to historic and orthodox Christianity. It is included in all of the great creeds. Athanasius is honored as the great defender of this truth against those who would degrade Christ to half creature and half God. He declared Christ to be inseparable from God as light is inseparable from fire or as the stream of water is inseparable from the fountain. Light is not fire and fire is not light, but they are of the same substance, just as a ray from the sun is composed of the same elements as the sun and yet it is not the sun. Thus the same water which comes from the fountain forms the stream, but the stream is not the fountain and the fountain is not the stream. Our statement of faith says, "We believe in the deity of our Lord Jesus Christ, in His virgin birth, in His sinless life, in His miracles, in His vicarious and atoning death through His shed blood, in His

34

bodily resurrection, in His ascension to the right hand of the Father, and in His personal return in power and glory."

This ancient and orthodox view is to be differentiated from the modern views of Jesus of Nazareth. A commonly accepted view of the deity of Jesus Christ is based upon the hypothesis of the divinity of all men. Christ is declared to be divine because all men are divine. This view is the result of evolution applied to religion. It takes the hypothesis of a developing humanity and declares that Jesus Christ was the unusual in that developing process. He is that to which all men aspire in developing religious consciousness, but instead of exalting man to be the object of worship this view degrades Christ to human stature where He does not deserve worship. All non-trinitarians are able to accept this kind of divinity of Jesus. Often the phrase "the divinity of Jesus" is used to confuse real believers on the essential deity of Christ which non-trinitarians do not believe.

Another modern view declares that Jesus became identified with God through His religion and that by our practice of the religion of Jesus we may have the same religious experience and thus also become divine. This view does not qualitatively separate the deity of Jesus Christ from the divinity of men. On the other hand Biblical Christianity presents to us a religion about Jesus in which He became the object of our worship because He is uniquely God.

Still another view from which we must differentiate the deity of Christ is the theory that Jesus is God because all is God and God is all. This is a basic pantheism based upon a spiritualistic monism. We are told that the world is spirit, that God is spirit and spirit is all. Jesus according to this theory realized His divinity, but we do not realize our divinity because we are in error. As we conquer our error we realize our spiritual unity with God. No comment is necessary to point out the gulf which separates this from Biblical teaching concerning the deity of Christ.

The Christian view of the deity of Christ is delineated in our worship. We Christians worship Jesus Christ as the object of our faith. To worship a creature or anything less than God is idolatry, no matter how elevated that creature may be. This is illustrated by the experience of John the Beloved in his apocalyptic vision. He said, "When I had heard and seen, I fell down and worshipped before the feet of the angel which showed me these things. Then saith he unto me, See thou do it not: for I am thy fellow servant . . . worship God." No creature is worthy of worship.

A confession of the deity of Christ is delineated in our relationship to Him. Jesus Christ is Lord, unique, unparalleled, exalted and the object of our faith. We have a servant-master relationship to Him. We never place Him on the level of the creature.

Our faith in Jesus Christ is declared by our confession which involves areas in which the God-Man is utterly different from any other man in history. Each of these declares Jesus of Nazareth to be the Christ of God. Each of the topics merits a full dissertation, but we can only refer to the series briefly at this time.

I. THE VIRGIN BIRTH

The deity of Christ was manifested by His virgin birth which was the means of the incarnation of God in human flesh. In Jesus of Nazareth God assumed flesh, entered this world, experienced time, space and relationship to material things, none of which could be postulated of Him before the incarnation. Far from being one of many incarnations, Christianity believes this to be the only incarnation. Here alone God became real man. There are many legends from mythology of the love affairs of the gods with the daughters of men, but these are so far below the level of the virgin birth of Jesus Christ that they are Satanic counterfeits which attempt to discredit the incarnation of Deity. That which is affirmed of Christ in the Scriptures could apply to none but Deity. The eternal Word became flesh. He is declared to be with God, to be God, to manifest the Father and to be of eternity. In Jesus Christ we have the invisible God become visible before men.

That incarnation took place by a miraculous birth from a virgin. The virgin birth is clearly and unequivocably taught in the Bible. Luke I tells us that the power of the highest over-shadowed the virgin Mary and the holy thing that was born was the Son of God. Jesus was born of a virgin mother without a human father. This fact brings us face to face with the supernatural. The virgin birth is a device to bring about the God-Man. It is not a device invented on the part of men, but the product of the infinite wisdom of God. In Jesus there was the infinite nature of Deity and the blood of Deity, for the blood of any child is received from his father and not from his mother. Since Jesus was without a human father, infinite value is imparted to the blood of this God-Man. Jesus derived the nature and flesh of man from His mother Mary. If the Saviour were to be of essential deity and without sin a virgin birth was the only possible way in which He could come into the world. We are aware that there are those who hold this to be non-essential, but if the virgin birth is not a part of the experience of Jesus Christ we could hardly declare Him to be unique diety.

The virgin birth produced what Simeon called the apparatus of salvation. Jesus Christ is true God in the source of life. Hence an infinite being, sufficient in value for all men. Moreover, He is true man in nature received from Mary and therefore adequate to represent men.

There is no fiction about the reality of His humanity or the reality of His deity. He had two natures in one person. Only such a being could become the Mediator, the Substitute and the Redeemer of men. Thus it was when Simeon held the baby Jesus in his arms, he said, "Now lettest thou thy servant depart in peace for mine eyes have seen thy salvation." The word salvation is in the neuter, referring to the apparatus of salvation. It was by this God-Man that salvation was destined to be wrought for the human race.

II. THE SINLESS LIFE OF JESUS CHRIST

When we declare that we believe in the sinless life of Christ we are speaking of its perfection. The definition of perfection depends upon our definition of sin, but no matter what your definition of sin, Christ is still perfect, and such perfection cannot be postulated of men.

Christ was perfect according to the law. He said concerning the law, "Think not that I am come to destroy the law . . . I am not come to destroy, but to fulfil." Christ was blameless according to the law under which He lived. Paul said He was "made of a woman, made under the law." The writer of Hebrews describes Him as "without spot." Jesus could challenge His enemies to convict Him of any sin. According to the law He was presented in the temple and He submitted to the rite of baptism saying, "Suffer it to be so now: for thus it becometh us to fulfil all righteousness." Jesus Christ carried the curse of the law judicially, for it is written, "Christ hath redeemed us from the curse of the law, being made a curse for us." However, ethically and morally He was free from transgression of the law.

Jesus Christ yielded a perfect obedience unto the Father. There was no lack of conformity to the law or to

the will of God, even unconsciously, in the life of Christ.
This is the testimony of the Scripture. The angel said,
"That holy thing which shall be born shall be called the
Son of God." Christ said, "The prince of this world cometh, and hath nothing in me." The writer of Hebrews
declares, "He was in all points tempted like as we are yet
without sin." John the Beloved wrote, "Ye know that he
was manifested to take away our sins; and in him is no
sin." He gave active obedience unto God. He is described
as saying to the Father when He came into the world, "Lo,
I come to do Thy will, O God." When He was teaching
the people, He said, "For I came down from heaven, not
to do mine own will, but the will of him that sent me."
Christ actively obeyed God. He never joined His disciples
in praying, "Forgive us our sins," and never made a confession of moral error. He yielded a passive obedience when
He endured the shame of the cross which was brought
upon Him by His enemies. Thus the Scripture says, "For
he (God) hath made him to be sin for us, who knew no
sin; that we might be made the righteousness of God in
him." Peter joins His sinlessness with His sacrifice saying,
"Who did no sin . . . who his own self bare our sins in his
own body on the tree."

Christ also was the perfect ideal of humanity. It is
in this sense that "The Son of Man" as a title is conferred
upon Him, for it intimates that He answers to the perfect
ideal of humanity. The Scripture portrays Him as an
ideal man. The writer of Hebrews tells us that He fulfills
the description of the ideal man in the Second Psalm saying, "But we see Jesus, who was made a little lower than
the angels by the suffering of death, crowned with glory
and honer." Paul declared, "The first man Adam was made
a living soul; the last Adam was made a quickening spirit."
Jesus was able to say to His disciples, "Whosoever will
come after me, let him deny himself, take up his cross and

follow me." Only the ideal man could say "Follow me." He is the standard. By the Spirit we "are changed into the same image from glory to glory." And He "shall change our vile body, that it may be fashioned like unto his own glorious body." Christ is the perfect man, the ideal man.

III. The Miracles of Jesus Christ

The deity of Christ is manifested by His miracles. The apostles appealed to the record of His miracles as evidence of His deity. Peter said at Pentecost, "Ye men of Israel, hear these words; Jesus of Nazareth, a man approved of God among you by miracles and wonders and signs, which God did by him in the midst of you, as ye yourselves know." Such miracles, wonders and signs were startling, supernatural, significant works performed by Christ Jesus which amazed the people. They may be separated into works pertaining to mental imbalance, to physical sickness or to the controlling elements of the world, but over all these things He exercised absolute power. That supernatural aspect of His nature is strongly attested in the incarnation and the resurrection, but the miracles wrought by Him give further evidence that He was approved of God.

They witnessed to His person. Jesus said, "Believe me for the very works sake." These mighty wonders, miracles and signs are a constituent part of the evidence that Jesus of Nazareth was the Son of God. Obviously, the miracles alone would not establish Him as the Son of God, but when taken in conjunction with the whole picture of Christ as pre-existent, fulfilling prophecy, virgin born, living in sinless life and ultimately rising from the dead, they add evidence to the whole proof of His deity. The miracles, of course, are historically validated by the kind of person which Christ was, for if He had been an evil person using His miracles for His own glory, the presumption would be against them. The alternatives must be faced that miracles declare the messenger to be from God or Satan, but at least they involve the operations of laws unknown to the average individual.

These miracles manifested His power and reemphasized that such power was always going out from Him. The Bible declares that creation was by Him. "By him were all things made that were made and without him was not anything made that was made." And again, "All things were made for him and by him." He is the executor of the Godhead in the sustaining of the universe through providence and if He has the providential sustaining of the universe, why should He not have special providences in the form of miracles? Even the healing processes of the human body are natural processes, but they may be speeded up by the Giver of all life. All of these, however they may be explained, are miracles of Christ.

IV. THE VICARIOUS DEATH OF JESUS CHRIST

We believe . . . in the vicarious and atoning death through His shed blood.

The shed blood represents the sacrifice of the Cross. To this we attach no value because of martyrdom or the moral example of love or the manifestation of governmental law in action. The value of the shed blood of Christ is in giving divine life which was in the blood as an atonement for the souls of men. That blood was shed and left in this world for our sins. It is the only thing that Christ did not take back to glory with Him. The shedding of His blood involved the suffering of the Cross in all of its cruelty, ignominy, shame and despicable aspects.

This shedding of blood was "atoning." That means

that is was a death on account of and for sin. God's justice was satisfied in the death of the Lamb of God. The life is in the blood. God has given us the blood for a sacrifice upon the altar. It was the blood of the perfect God-Man incarnate Deity, shed upon the Cross that made a sufficient satisfaction for our sins. From this sacrifice the sins of the world are forgiven in accordance with divine justice. God was in Christ reconciling the world unto Himself, not imputing their trespasses unto them.

This sacrifice was vicarious, that is, a substitution for others. To say that it was vicarious adds nothing to what the Scripture says, for the Scripture tells us that Christ died for sinners. "All we like sheep have gone astray. We have turned every one to his own way and the Lord hath laid upon him the iniquity of us all," for "he hath made him to be sin for us, who knew no sin; that we might be made the righteousness of God in him." This infinite sacrifice was sufficient for all who believed. Christ took their place literally and effectively. What a wonderful realization that this sacrifice was for me and that it was my sin that sent Him to Calvary. If Christ had died for no one else, He would have died for me. He "loved me, and gave himself for me."

V. The Bodily Resurrection

It is the plain teaching of Scripture that Christ rose from the dead. Paul said, "I delivered unto you . . . that which I also received, how that Christ died for our sins according to the Scriptures; and that he was buried and that he rose again the third day according to the Scriptures." There is evidence from the Old Testament that Christ was to rise from the dead. In appeal to this, Peter quoted the Sixteenth Psalm written by David in which he said, "Neither wilt thou suffer thine Holy One to see corruption" which is applied unto the death and resurrection of Jesus Christ. Christ Himself made many prophecies concerning His death and resurrection, beginning at the time of His transfiguration and continuing until His death. Concerning these Matthew says, "From that time forth began Jesus to show unto his disciples, how he must go unto Jerusalem, and suffer many things of the elders and chief priests and scribes, and be killed, and be raised again the third day." Until the death and resurrection of Christ the New Testament apostles did not understand it, but in their subsequent writing the New Testament abundantly declares the resurrection of Christ from the dead.

The proof of reason attests this resurrection and to it we may logically appeal. There are psychological proofs in the tranformation of the disciples.

There are historical proofs in the appearances of the resurrection Christ. There are logical proofs in the open tomb which are able to convince an unprejudiced mind concerning the resurrection of Christ. An illustration of this may be given in the conversion of two of England's most brilliant men who in the days of the triumph of deism denied the supernatural. They were the eminent legal authorities Gilbert West and Lord Lyttleton. These two men who were put forward to crush the defenders of the supernatural in the Bible had a conference together. One of them said to the other that it would be difficult to maintain their position unless they disposed of two of the alleged bulwarks of Christianity, namely, the alleged resurrection of Jesus from the dead and the alleged conversion of Saul of Tarsus. Lyttleton undertook to write a book to show that Saul of Tarsus was never converted as is recorded in the Acts of the Apostles, but that his alleged conversion was a myth, if Gilbert West would write another book to show that the alleged resurrection of Christ was a myth. West said to Lyttleton, "I shall have to depend upon you for my facts for I am somewhat rusty in the Bible," to which Lyttleton replied that he was counting upon West, for he was somewhat rusty in the Bible. One of them said to the other, "If we are to be honest in the matter, we ought at least to study the evidence," and this they undertook to do. They had numerous conferences together while preparing their work. In one of the conferences West said to Lyttleton that there had been something in his mind for sometime that he thought he ought to speak to him about. As he had been studying the evidence, he was beginning to feel that there was something in it. Lyttleton replied that he was glad that he had spoken about it, for he, too, was somewhat shaken, as he had been studying the evidence for the conversion of Saul of Tarsus. Finally, when the books were finished the two men met. West said to Lyttleton, "Have you written your book?" He replied that he had, but he said, "West, as I have been studying the evidence and weighing it by the recognized laws of legal evidence, I have become satisfied that Saul of Tarsus was converted as is stated in the Acts of the Apostles, and that Christianity is true, and I have written my book on that side." The book can be found today in first class libraries. "Well," said West, "as I have studied the evidence for the resurrection of Jesus Christ from the dead, and have weighed it according to the acknowledged laws of evidence, I have become really satisfied that Jesus really rose from the dead as recorded in the Gospels, and have written my book on that side." This book can also be found in our libraries today. If you have questions in your mind about this subject, take the great evidence of the open tomb and reason from it to the deity of Christ.

It is this truth which has the power to comfort, for it declares unto us that we are not in our sins and Christianity is true. It declares that we shall see our loved ones again and death is not the end. It tells us that our bodies shall rise from the dead and we shall know an individual immortality.

VI. The Ascension of Jesus Christ

We believe . . . in His ascension to the right hand of the Father. This describes the place of triumph. The victory of Christ on Calvary is differentiated from His triumph in the heavenlies. It was the victory, not the triumph, which cost the blood, the sweat and the tears. But the victory deserves the triumph and the triumph came before the heavenly hosts in honor, acknowledging Christ's attainment. In the triumph He made an open show of His enemies, as Colossians 2:15 tells us. The spoils of victory were in His hands. He took the keys of death and hell and He became the Lord of His people.

Christ ascended to the place of intercession, for He ever liveth to make intercession for us. There He entered upon His eternal priesthood as advocate and divine helper. That was the beginning of His mediatorial kingdom as priest-king over His people and in that intercession He guarantees the security of His people through His own prayers. What He said to Peter may be said to us, "I have prayed for thee that thy faith fail not." Thank God for the prayers of our great Intercessor.

The place of triumph was the place of power. From there He exercises sovereignty. In His resurrection form He said, "All authority in heaven and earth is given to me." He has been exalted to the right hand of the Father, above all principalities and powers and every name that is named. There He has the restored glory which was His before the foundation of the world, comparable to the glory seen on the Mount of Transfiguration which Peter described as "his majesty."

VII. The Personal Return

This same Jesus will come again from heaven whence He ascended. The message was proclaimed by the angels on the Mount of Olives when they said, " . . . this same Jesus which is taken up from you . . . shall so come in like manner as ye have seen him go into heaven." This was promised by the Lord Himself when He said, "Then shall appear the sign of the Son of Man in heaven . . . and they shall see the Son of man coming in the clouds of heaven with power and great glory." This doctrine was preached by the apostles who said, "Whom (Christ) the heaven must receive until the times of the restitution of all things." And "He hath appointed a day, in the which he will judge the world in righteousness by that man whom he hath ordained." And "The Lord Jesus shall be revealed from heaven with his mighty angels, in flaming fire taking vengeance on them that know not God."

His coming is the counterpart of His humiliation. In that day every eye shall see Him and recognize Him and acknowledge Him as the Son of God and King of kings. Then every man shall be judged by Him for He said, "In that day ye shall say unto me." Every nation and people shall be subject unto Him for He shall be King of kings and Lord of lords and the kingdoms of this world will become the kingdoms of our Lord and His Christ.

The personal coming of the Lord Jesus is imminent. There is no major item today which delays the event. It is possible that He may come at any hour. It is this which is the incentive to watchfulness on the part of His people and to the fulfillment of those commands which He has laid upon them. This is the crowning event of the historical process of the redemptive deeds of God. Jesus Christ is coming again.

CHAPTER IV

THE AGENT OF GOD

Except a man be born of water and of the Spirit he cannot enter into the kingdom of God (John 3:3).

The deity of the Holy Spirit is clearly taught in the Bible. As one of the persons of the Trinity the Spirit shares identity of essence or being. Hence the Spirit is variously called, "The Spirit of Christ" and "The Spirit of God" and "The Holy Spirit" and the name of God is the name of "The Father, the Son, and the Holy Spirit." To the Holy Spirit are given divine attributes, honors and worship. To lie to the Holy Spirit is to lie to God. To reject the ministry of the Holy Spirit is to reject the ministry of God. To pray unto the Holy Spirit is to pray unto God and to possess the Holy Spirit is to possess God.

The Father, Son and Holy Spirit exist simultaneously and not successively. It has often been affirmed that God manifested Himself first in the Father, then as Son and finally as the Holy Spirit and that His manifestation as Son did not occur until He ceased to manifest Himself as Father and the manifestation as The Spirit did not occur until He ceased to manifest Himself as Son. This theory of the successive manifestation of one God is a form of the ancient error called Modalism, which states that there are three manifestations of the Godhead and not three persons in the Godhead. It is clear from the Bible that the Spirit, the Son and the Father all exist and work simultaneously. Both the Son and Spirit are declared to have a part in the creation. The Son declares that the Father and He will come and take up His abode with the believer. The Son addresses the Father as Thou and the

47

Father addresses the Son as Thou. The Holy Spirit testifies of the Son and is said to proceed from the Father and the Son.

The Spirit's presence in the world makes God's presence just as real as it was when Christ was on earth. They called Christ Immanuel, God with us. But the Holy Spirit may also be called Immanuel, for He is God with us. Christ speaks of Him as "another Comforter," a divine helper given to the individual. Your experience of the nearness of God, and of His power and blessing depends on the Holy Spirit. Only in Him God is present and active. When Christ promised the presence of another comforter who would guide into all truth He declared the agency of the Spirit acting for the Godhead.

The personality of the Holy Spirit is also clearly declared. There is an unfortunate practice in the church of impersonalizing the Holy Spirit as a force, a power or an influence. This degrades the Spirit to a nebulous and mysterious atmosphere, rather than an active agent to whom the work of the church is committed. Christ was very careful in His practice of attributing exalted personality to the Spirit. He said, "I will pray the Father and he shall give you another Comforter, that he may abide with you forever; even the Spirit of truth; whom the world cannot receive, because it seeth him not, neither knoweth him: but ye know him; for he dwelleth with you, and shall be in you . . . Howbeit when he, the Spirit of truth is come, he will guide you into all truth: for he shall not speak of himself; for whatsoever he shall hear, that shall he speak: and he will show you things to come. He shall glorify me: for he shall receive of mine, and show it unto you." Christ affirms that the Spirit speaks, teaches, guides, helps, comforts and performs other activities of personality. In history whenever the church practiced giving the proper place to the Holy Spirit, it received great blessing. Whenever revivals occurred, they came through the ministration of the Holy Spirit.

The work of the Holy Spirit is defined in Scripture by the Lord Jesus. He said He would send Him and also prayed that the Father would send Him which gives justification for the Spirit coming from the Father and the Son. This work of the Spirit includes convicting of sin, especially the sin of unbelief. Without the conviction of the Holy Spirit, conversion through the ministry of the Word would not be possible. It includes convincing of righteousness, and teaching the divinely prepared way of salvation. God is shown to be righteous and able to make sinful men righteous because Christ is righteous. Natural reasoning would never arrive at this conclusion. It must be brought about through the convincing power of the Holy Spirit. He must convince men of judgment, and that they will be held accountable for every deed. Every wrong shall be righted and every evil shall be compensated at the judgment. All this work of the Holy Spirit began at Pentecost, when He made His advent as comforter, advocate and agent of the Godhead. Peter said of Christ, "Being by the right hand of God exalted, and having received of the Father the promise of the Holy Ghost, he hath shed forth this, which ye now see and hear." That was the fulfillment of Christ's own promise of the coming of the Holy Ghost.

Let us consider the work and person of the Holy Spirit from these points of view: applied salvation, experiential salvation and practical salvation.

I. Applied Salvation — Justification

To be "lost" is to be away from the known, to be off center, wandering, a prodigal, away from home. It implies a departure, a fall and its result. All that is expressed in the parables of the lost sheep, the lost coin, and the lost son is applicable here. A child is lost in the woods or in a great city. Panic, fear and strangeness descend upon him and unless he is found and rescued, he would never find his way back. This is also true of a lost soul.

The word "sinful" refers to the present state of man. He is both potentially and actually guilty. Man has sinned, but that did not make him a sinner. He was a sinner by nature. Even when man's guilt is removed for the actual sins he committed, he still retains the potential guilt of his sinful nature. A saved man is a sinner saved by grace, but he is still a sinner. Not that he actually commits sin, but he has a sinful nature.

In the eighth Psalm the psalmist expresses his conception of an ideal man. There he declares that man was created, is to be exalted above the angels and to be given sovereignty over all things. This is Christian anthropology. That man was created in God's image but is lost and sinful is not a popular conception, however, it is Biblical.

Salvation was settled objectively by Christ on the Cross. That work of Christ was done in history. The Holy Spirit does not accomplish this phase of salvation. It is finished. Nothing can be added to it. The Father did not endure the pain of judgment on Calvary any more than the Spirit accomplished our salvation. It was the Lamb of God, even the Lord Jesus Christ, who died upon the Cross and is the unique Saviour and the Redeemer of men.

That salvation is sufficient for humanity. Christ is "The Saviour of all men, especially those that believe." And "God was in Christ, reconciling the world unto himself, not imputing their trespasses unto them." The infinite and eternal Son of God purchased our salvation by His terrible sufferings upon the Cross. His death was sufficient for all men.

Christ's death was a satisfaction to God. God's righteousness is satisfied because death which is the wages of sin has been atoned for by an infinite being, Jesus Christ. God, being reconciled and favorably disposed, offers grace and mercy so that the believing sinner is justified in His sight. This is no fiction, no trickery or legerdemain, but a reality through Jesus Christ. God accepted what Christ did for sinners. There is salvation for lost and sinful men.

This does not guarantee individual deliverance from sin. Our salvation which is the work of Christ must be effectively applied to individuals or it would be in vain. Hypothetically, the great objective finished atonement could have occurred without the salvation of individuals. The application of salvation to individuals is the work of the Spirit. The Holy Spirit calls, convicts, justifies, regenerates, preserves, and glorifies the individual. The available blessings are applied by him. No preacher, no man can do this essentially divine work. All soul winning is ineffectual unless it is done with dependence on and trust in the Holy Spirit the agent of the Godhead in individual salvation.

The individual therefore is saved by the work of the Holy Spirit. He applies redemption and makes it personal. There is no work of God without the Spirit. How the Holy Spirit does this, on whom He works and with what degree of irresistible power, are questions we cannot answer. Denominational differences arise from different emphases on the work of the Spirit. It is not our province to enter into them now.

II. EXPERIENTIAL SALVATION — REGENERATION

Regeneration is an experience, rather than a doctrine. The great criticism of fundamentalism is that Christianity is limited too much to the historical, objective, dogmatic truth without a carry-over into life. The movement called

Fundamentalism has been too much concerned with orthodoxy and too little concerned with life. Christians have
been counted by giving assent to a system of truth rather
than by experiencing new birth. Dead orthodoxy can be
as great a reproach to Christianity as unbelief. The tragedy
is that character transformation has not occurred in the
proportion which it should have occurred. The carry over
is lacking. The cross has not become a way of life. It is
merely a philosophy to be accepted.

The Bible, however, presents the challenge of Christian
experience. It speaks of the sense of guilt, condemnation
and enmity being removed from the conscience by regeneration. Is it removed from you? It speaks of the assurance of forgiveness, acceptance in Christ, and inheritance
of life. Do you have that? It speaks of the desire to do
God's will which translates itself into action, so that a real
change occurs in character and conduct. Has that
occurred in your life?

Consider the conversion of St. Paul and the mighty
subjective change which was wrought in him at conversion. The conversion of St. Paul stands as one of the
greatest evidences of the truth of Christianity. Why is it
that we have so few conversions as definite, effective and
powerful in testimony as St. Paul's? It is largely because
we keep regeneration in the realm of thinking rather than
in the realm of experience.

Let us examine this doctrine of regeneration. The
authority for it is the Lord Jesus Christ. It was He who
announced it to Nicodemus and set the phrase used by
John, Paul, and all Christians. Christ expected Nicodemus
to understand the meaning of the doctrine of regeneration
as He taught it, for He said, "Art thou a master of Israel
and knowest not these things?" It had been taught in
ancient Israel that circumcision of the flesh was not circumcision, but only that which was circumcision of the

heart. There must be a regenerate experience, a new heart given to a man, and in the story of Nicodemus, Christ presented to a religious, educated, cultured, and representative man the definite teaching concerning regeneration. Were it not so explicit in the teaching of Christ and repeated by the apostles, one might be tempted to waive it from emphasis and trust to education for the transformation of men, but we cannot circumvent the authority of Jesus Christ.

He presented plain conditions for regeneration. He said, "Except a man be born of water and of the Spirit, he cannot see the kingdom of God." Water meant repentance then and it means repentance now, for it is a symbol of that. Thus St. Peter could say, "Repent and be baptized in the name of the Lord Jesus Christ and ye shall receive the gift of the Holy Ghost."

Repentance is a human experience and is within human power therefore the call to repentance must be met by the one to be born again. Next, Christ said, "Believe." He said, "He that believeth on me, as the Scripture hath said, out of his belly shall flow rivers of living water." John adds that by this He referred to the Holy Ghost who was not yet given. Also, Christ said, "Come unto me." When an individual is ready to repent, believe and come to Christ, there will be no question about the occurrence of his regeneration.

The result promised by Christ was life. He said "He that believeth on me hath everlasting life." He also said, "Whosoever believeth in him should not perish, but have everlasting life" and "I am come that they might have life." Another result is the knowledge of God, for Christ said, "If ye had known me ye should have known my Father also." Another result is freedom from condemnation, for Christ said, "He that believeth on him is not condemned: but he that believeth not, is condemned already."

As we seek to explain regeneration, we are confronted with Christ's own statement, "Marvel not that I said unto you, ye must be born again. The wind bloweth where it listeth, thou hearest the sound thereof, but canst not tell whence it cometh, and whither it goeth: so is every one that is born of the Spirit." In other words, regeneration is a mystery. It is wrought by an act of God, the laws of which we know but we cannot fathom the origin. The wind makes a perfect illustration. The weather man may chart the highs and the lows of weather changes. He may know the directions of the wind and chart them, but he does not know the causes of those atmospheric changes. They remain a mystery. Likewise the natural life remains a mystery. We may know the laws that control it and may experiment with them, but we never know the source of life itself.

Yet it is defined as a new creation. "If any man be in Christ, he is a new creature: old things are passed away; behold, all things are become new." There is something added, something given, something not possessed before involved in this new nature, new principle, and new life. It is the explanation of the utter and complete change in the individual, as old things pass away and all things become new. A new creation has occurred within the individual.

The Bible describes this as the gift of the Holy Spirit. Peter says, "Repent, and be baptized in the name of Jesus Christ for the remission of sins, and ye shall receive the gift of the Holy Ghost." God gives Himself in the form of the Third Person of the Trinity, the Holy Spirit, the Witness, the Seal, the Earnest of our inheritance, when we meet the conditions of regeneration. It is the life of God in us which we receive as the divine gift through the agency of the Holy Spirit.

III. PRACTICAL SALVATION — TRANSFORMATION

The Holy Spirit indwells the believer. The reception of the Holy Spirit occurs at our new birth or our regeneration. Romans 8:9 says, "If any man have not the Spirit of Christ, he is none of his." We cannot be Christians without the Holy Spirit. If a man is a true Christian, he has the Holy Spirit. The Holy Spirit is not able to be divided because He is a personality. Therefore, man has all there is of the Holy Spirit, although the Holy Spirit may not yet dominate and control him.

The Holy Spirit is the reservoir of all divine blessing and He is within us. Paul speaks of the "By the Spirit blessings." Since Pentecost every Christian is united with Christ and with other Christians by the Holy Spirit. As a Christian he has access unto the divine reservoir of blessings which are in Christ Jesus through the Spirit.

The Christian must realize the spiritual privileges of having the Holy Spirit in one. This demands our surrender, obedience and trust, for the Holy Ghost is given to them that obey Him and we are to grieve not the Spirit of God. Therefore, our complete surrender is essential. Such a realization will bring us power, for after the Holy Ghost is come upon us we will have power. It will bring us victory, for this is the victory that overcometh the world and it will bring us assurance, for He is the witness of our salvation. The realization of our spiritual privilege will correspond to the state of our souls. Is the Holy Spirit first and exalted in your life? Then your blessings will be correspondent.

Regeneration introduces the Holy Spirit to our lives, but His ministry does not end there. He continues to illuminate our understanding and reveal the Christ to us. It is the Holy Spirit's ministry to teach us the truth of the Word which cannot be grasped by the natural man. It is

His business to guide us into the divine will, designate the fields of service, pray for us lest we should sin and preserve us from all evil.

Such a ministry is needed in every day living. Only this ministry of the Spirit will deliver us from the besetting sins of the old man. Only the Holy Spirit can renew our minds after Christ's image of holiness. Truly godly lives are at a premium and they can only be lived through the ministry and indwelling of the Holy Spirit.

This ministry of the Spirit does not end until we become like Christ. "We all, with open face beholding as in a glass the glory of the Lord, are changed into the same image from glory to glory, even as by the Spirit of the Lord." The work of the Holy Spirit is to transform us according to God's plan, renew our minds that we may prove what is the good, acceptable and perfect will of God.

Men of the Spirit or men dominated by the Holy Spirit are the men whom God uses. They are described in the Bible as "moved by the Holy Ghost." They are under His dominion, His control and His will. He is able to direct them, empower them, enlighten them, and use them according to His purposes. Today the greatest opportunity of all time opens for Christians "filled with" and "anointed by" and "empowered" by the Holy Spirit. Oh that God could put His hand on a group of men to whom He could entrust the blessing of the Holy Spirit in His fullness. To grasp for the best that God has for us is no ambition. It is commendable. We are not to be satisfied with a divided life, defeated souls and discouragement. We are to seek God's best, the fullness of His Holy Spirit and the manifestation of His presence and ministry in our lives.

By the agent of the Godhead, Christianity is revitalized. The gulf between the historical work of Christ and the experiential Christian life is closed. Dogma and deeds, creed and conduct become inseparable. The great emphasis of our life must be on the Holy Spirit who will exalt Christ and Calvary to us and thus manifest the Christian way.

CHAPTER V

THE PURPOSE OF GOD

The hour is coming, in the which all that are in the graves shall hear His voice, and shall come forth; they that have done good, unto the resurrection of life; and they that have done evil, unto the resurrection of damnation (John 5:28-29).

The purpose of God means the elective decrees of God involving predestination and salvation, and to this we shall limit it.

The difference between the saved and the lost is a differentiation made by God. God will finally settle the issue of whether a man is saved or lost. He alone has the authority and wisdom to do so, yet God is not arbitrary in His decrees nor does He do violence to the will of His creatures in the fulfillment of His purpose. That there are saved and lost is made abundantly clear in the Scripture. In Genesis we have the line of Seth and of Cain. In Psalm one we have the godly and the ungodly. In the New Testament we have the believers and the unbelievers. In Revelation there are those who are within the holy city and those who are without who will have their part in the lake which burneth with fire and brimstone. This distinction between the saved and the lost is the essence of Christianity. Before God created the world His divine foreknowledge enabled Him to know who would be saved and who would be lost and thus to predestinate all to their ultimate condition.

The Scripture also declares that it is the desire of God that all men be saved. He "will have all men to be saved, and to come to the knowledge of the truth." He is "not willing that any should perish, but that all should come to repentance." This is God's desire. That it is His desire was demonstrated in the fact that He sent His only-begotten Son to be a propitiation for the sins of the whole .world. No one debates that the death of the infinite and eternal Son of God was a sufficient atonement for all mankind, for Paul says, "God was in Christ, reconciling the world unto himself, not imputing their trespasses unto them." This is also implied in the universal commission to preach the Gospel and the universal command to repent. Christ told the disciples, "Go ye therefore, and teach all nations, baptizing them." And Paul said, "God . . . now commandeth all men everywhere to repent." It is certain from the Bible that it is the desire of God that all men shall be saved.

The decree of God does not coincide with His desire, however. The will of God expressing desire is stated in the New Testament by the Greek word *thelema,* whereas the will of God expressing decree is stated by the Greek word *boulema.* This distinction between the wills of God must never be forgotten. It is here that the shades of Calvin and Arminius enter the picture and it is here in my own understanding of Scripture that I diverge from true Calvinism. I believe the Bible teaches that the decree of God guarantees that only the believers shall be saved. That all are not saved is obvious both from Scripture and experience. Why is it that some are saved and not others? The Scripture universally declares that faith is the condition of salvation. Paul said, "Believe on the Lord Jesus Christ, and thou shalt be saved, and thy house." Also "Being justified by faith, we have peace with God." Also, "By grace are ye saved through faith; and that not of yourselves: it is the gift of God: not of works, lest any man should boast." Also, "God . . . is the Saviour of all men, specially of those that believe." When God elects to salvation only those who believe, it places ultimate responsibility upon the individual in accordance with the doctrine of predestination and the teaching of Scripture. Salvation is utterly of God. It has been completed upon the cross of Calvary. The exercise of faith is individual responsibility. It is altogether rational that God in accordance with His divine foreknowledge has predestined all believers to be saved.

I. THE RESURRECTION

Belief in the resurrection means that all men will rise from the dead. Jesus said, "All that are in the tombs, shall hear His voice and shall come forth." This contemplates the rising of the bodies of men from all kinds of graves. Daniel said, "Many of them that sleep in the dust of the earth shall awake" and John the beloved declared, "I saw the dead, small and great, stand before God." Also, "The sea gave up the dead that were in it; and death and hell delivered up the dead which were in them." The Scriptural teaching concerning the resurrection of the body could not mean the resurrection of a sleeping soul for there are too many Scriptural passages which forbid our believing in the sleep of the soul. Christ's statement to the thief on the Cross "This day thou shalt be with me in paradise" simply cannot be interpreted consistently with the sleep of the soul. Likewise St. Paul declared that "To be absent from the body" is "to be present with the Lord." Therefore, he desired to depart and "to be with Christ, which is far better." The text must mean a reviving of the body by a return of the soul.

There never was a question among Christians of whether they believed in the continued existence of the soul, but whether they believed in the resurrection of the body. It was for that purpose that St. Paul wrote the fifteenth chapter of First Corinthians. He assumed that they believed in the resurrection of Christ and the continued existence of the soul, but he was proving the resurrection of the body. We evangelicals believe in a bodily resurrection.

The affirmation of a resurrection, however, does not define the nature of the spiritual body, this "tabernacle not made with hands." No man can define the nature of the resurrection body. We know that it will be the same body, but with different qualities as St. Paul describes them in First Corinthians 15. Instead of being a natural body it will be spiritual. Instead of being weak, it will be powerful. Instead of being corruptible, it will be incorruptible. Instead of being humble, it will be glorious and these are only suggestions of what the resurrection body will be.

The time honored proof of the resurrection of the body is that Christ rose from the dead. Even in the last book which was printed on the question, "Can We Still Believe In Immortality?" the argument is not founded in scientific and philosophic arguments, though those have their place, but on the resurrection of Christ. Christ came from the tomb in the same body in which He was buried. The common consent of Christians to this is used in First Corinthians to prove the resurrection of the believer, for Christ was seen, handled, heard and known as He appeared after His resurrection. His body was actually gone from the tomb and it was the same body though changed. The entire teaching of Scripture is that our resurrection body will be like His. We shall be "changed." We shall be made like unto Him. We shall bear His image and to do this there must be a resurrection body.

The purpose of a bodily resurrection is to receive for the deeds done in the body. Resurrection is the restoration of the complete personality. The sins of life such as unbelief, rejection of Christ and overt acts contrary to God's law were committed in the body and we must answer for such sins. We will be judged "for the deeds done in the body." Similarly the rewards of things done in the body in this life must be received in the body. It is only by a resurrection of the body that humanity will reach the destiny for which it was created. The body is no illusion. It is not something to be sloughed off. It is a divinely intended blessing and redeemed it will be wonderful beyond the imagination of man. For this reason Paul said, "The whole creation groaneth and travaileth in pain together until now. And not only they, but ourselves also, which have the first fruits of the Spirit, even we ourselves groan within ourselves, waiting for the adoption, to-wit, the redemption of our body."

II. The Resurrection of Life

I understand the Scripture to teach that the resurrection of life will occur at the coming of the Lord Jesus Christ. Certainly it is declared in First Thessalonians, "If we believe that Jesus died and rose again, even so them also which sleep in Jesus will God bring with him . . . for the Lord himself shall descend from heaven with a shout, with the voice of an archangel, and with the trump of God: and the dead in Christ shall rise first." Here is a shout which will awaken the dead and they shall come to life. There are some who believe that all dead, the righteous and the wicked, will rise at once, but it is obvious that the text speaks of "the resurrection of life" and "the resurrection of damnation." The same kind of division is made in the twentieth chapter of Revelation. Certainly it seems that there is a millennium intervening between these two resurrections. But there are many Christians who do not believe there are two future resurrections, not because they do not believe the Bible but because they identify the first resurrection with the resurrection from being dead in trespasses and in sins.

The resurrection of life is for participation in God's glory. Christ will come as King of kings and will subdue His enemies. He is now seated at the right hand of the Father, "expecting until His enemies be made His footstool." That coming will be the consummation of His mediatorial work. It will be glorious, powerful and victorious and Christians are to share that glory as the bride of Christ, as sovereign over His heritage and coheirs with Him of the divine inheritance. This is the regeneration and restoration of all things promised by the prophets. Christ assured His disciples that they would have a share in that regeneration. The restoration of all things is contingent upon Christ's coming again. In this resurrection of life Christian life will reach its flood tide by mystical union with the glorified Lord. This is the culmination of redemption for us. The resurrection life will be shared because we have a body like unto His body. This is the promise. We are to be "conformed to the image of his Son." We are to be "like him; for we shall see him as he is." We are to be "changed into the same image from glory to glory." All this was included in the redemption purchased at Calvary, but it will become an actuality in the resurrection of our bodies. Redemption from sickness, suffering and pain will be complete. The full effects of death will be removed. The possession of such a body will mean the privilege of unlimited activities in this glorious universe with the effects of sin removed. That leaves nothing to be desired. David described those pleasures as "pleasures forevermore." Such resurrection of life is the refined, indescribable joy of full expression of the personality in accordance with a good heart. That is heaven.

III. THE RESURRECTION OF DAMNATION

The lost will also be raised, but for them it will be a resurrection of damnation. This is the other side of the

picture. The purpose of such a resurrection is the punishment of evil doers. God has unequivocally declared that a
future judgment will settle all unsettled accounts in this
world. Experience and history demand such a judgment
for the fulfillment of justice. If there were no future
judgment and rectification of wrongs the adage "eat, drink
and be merry; for tomorrow we die" would be true. Then
the living of the good life would be irrational in many
ways. Without a future judgment there would be no
justice in the story of John the Baptist and Herodias. Our
good or bad deeds were performed in the body and they
must be rewarded in the body. At the judgment of the
full personality there will be no excuse of the soul blaming the body or the body blaming the soul, for the personality will be complete. Grace will not operate after the
resurrection, for it exists only in the time of the Gospel.
Now is the time. This is the hour of decision. The future
is the hour of judgment and punishment. All the dead will
stand before the throne.

I pause here to exclude the possibility of annihilation
or restoration of the soul. These theories are merely ave-
nues of escape from the fact of eternal punishment. They
are held by several sects, but we hold them to be un-
biblical.

Those who believe in annihilation teach that man is a
dependent being, resting for his existence on God who can
put him out of existence whenever He desires. Stress is
laid upon a period of punishment followed by the destruction of the wicked. The question is not what God can do,
but what does God do according to His revelation? Scripture has destruction come simultaneously with judgment,
not after a period of punishment (II Thess. 1:9). If judgment is annihilation, how could it come later? It is
obvious from Matthew 25:46 that heaven and hell are of
the same duration, for we have everlasting destruction and

everlasting life. If destruction, death and eternal punishment are synonymous, how can one believe in annihilation? In the tenth chapter of Matthew, the twenty-eighth verse, "destroy both soul and body" is used. The annihilationists tell us this means annihilation, but if we substitute the word annihilation for the word destroy or destruction in the thirty-ninth verse, the whole meaning becomes absurd.

The restorationists tell us that there is a temporary period of punishment after which the soul will be restored to purity and bliss. They say the Lord will devise means to restore His banished. Philosophically that is nice and it would be easy for us to believe, but it is unscriptural. It may be comforting to be a Universalist, but it cuts the nerve of evangelism and missions. In the Bible we are told that whoever rejects Christ sustains irreparable loss.

The resurrection of damnation, then, involves eternity. There is no second chance, for the destiny of the soul is settled at death. Life and death, with death involving eternal punishment, are of equal duration in the Scriptural teaching. The terrible and forbidding fact of that second death should compel us to attempt to escape that death with all our zeal. Only an infinite sin against the well-being of God and the universe could demand such a punishment. Eternal damnation is a terrible thought, but it is a Biblical teaching. With the possibility of eternal damnation it is impossible to connect an arbitrary decree consigning certain lost men to such a state. For me it is only possible to believe that God decreed their damnation because they would not believe.

The most important resurrection for us, however, is the present spiritual resurrection by which God unites us with Christ, raises us up with Him and sets us in heavenly places in Christ Jesus. If He has quickened us by His great love and mercy and through faith we have been saved, we need not fear the resurrection of damnation.

CHAPTER VI

THE UNITY OF THE CHURCH

Christ also loved the church, and gave himself for it (Eph. 5:25).
Christ . . . loved me, and gave himself for me (Gal. 2:20).

The texts emphasize the two poles of Christian experience — the corporate and the individual. Christ died for the church; and Christ died for me.

The seventeenth chapter of John concerns the redeemed. The redeemed are gathered in the Church. The paradox is: The Church is one now; the Church must become one. We face the absurdity on the one hand of two hundred and fifty or more denominations, many of which claim to be the true church. The genius of Protestantism is recognized as the belief in the infallibility of the Bible as the ultimate authority, the belief in salvation by the justification of the individual soul through faith and that alone, and the belief in the right of the private interpretation of the Scripture; yet Protestantism has now gone into the extreme of division ad infinitum. On the other hand, we face the schism of Romanism in its bigoted claim to be the only church. The literature of the Paulist fathers, prepared for the non-Catholic, is constantly harping upon this string. We are told that there is only one true Church, that all other churches are not churches at all and that the Roman Church is the Church of Jesus Christ. The time has come for some clear thinking concerning the Church, its nature, its unity, its voice and its existence.

We are faced with the following contrast: There is no salvation outside the Church, for Christ died for the Church. Also there is no salvation except by individual justification, for Christ died for the individuals. Both are true, but both have led to extremes of overemphasis. On the one hand we have the overemphasis of Romanism in stating that there is no salvation outside the Church and identifying the Church with an organization. On the other hand, there is the overemphasis of Protestantism which leads to an excessive fragmentization of the Church in organizational matters.

Therefore, let us bear in mind certain distinctions. First, there is the distinction between the Church organization and the Church organism. It was concerning the organism that Christ said, "On this rock I will build my church." It is concerning the organism that the Epistle to the Ephesians was written as an encyclical epistle to all churches. On the other hand, Matthew 18 was given to the Church organization in which there must be discipline, public teaching and prayer. It was concerning this Church organization that the Corinthian epistles were written in order to correct aberrations by discipline and to produce an organizational unity. We have, therefore, a particular and a universal Church, both of which are Scriptural. There is also the difference between what is called "The Church" and "Churches" or "asemblies." The Church is the Church universal, but the church at Boston or Pittsburgh or Chicago is an individual assembly, a particular congregation, still called a "Church." There is also a difference between the Church triumphant and Church militant. Those who have left this present scene of conflict have entered into the Church triumphant. Those believers who are still on earth are in the Church militant. There is no validity to the distinction between the visible and the invisible Church. Wherever the Church militant exists it must be visible. It is concerning the unity of the Church militant that we are writing.

I. CHRIST'S PRAYER FOR THE UNITY OF THE CHURCH

The passage of Scripture embraced in John 17:1-26 is called Christ's high-priestly prayer, His prayer for His Church. In it He prayed for all disciples, from those who believed on Him in that day to us and including the last believer who will commit his destiny to Jesus Christ in the temporal span. To them the Son of God gave eternal life, because they were given to Him by the Father. To them He manifested God's Name and Word and will and they whom the Father gave Him kept that Word. To them He revealed God's Word and they received and believed that Word. For such He prayed.

His fourfold petition consisted of the following: First, that the Father would keep those whom He had given to Christ, that they might be one as the Father and Christ are one. It was Christ's desire that the Father should keep them from the evil in the world. Second, He prayed that while they were in this world they might be sanctified through the Word of God which is the truth. For their sakes Christ had sanctified Himself as an example. Third, He prayed that they and all who would believe in Him might be one "as, thou, Father, art in me, and I in thee, that they also may be one in us." Fourth, He prayed that the Father would grant that they whom He had given Him might be with Him where He is and behold His glory.

The heart of this prayer is for the unity of all believers then existing and to come as a witness to the world, "That the world may believe that thou hast sent me."

We recall that it was the Son of God who prayed this prayer and we may be sure that the prayer was heard and answered for those disciples and is being answered for us today. They were kept except the one whom Christ called the son of perdition. They were sanctified by His Word; and they were ultimately taken to be with Him. So also they became one in Him. That unity was constituted at Pentecost. Then the individual stalks of grain were bound into a sheaf of grain. That was the beginning of the New Testament Church. The believers were baptized into one body or one organism. The Church, constituted of born-again, believing Christians has been spiritually one ever since Pentecost. There is this spiritual union of all believers in all branches of Christendom. There is only one Church and it is composed of such regenerated individuals in all nations, ecclesiastical organizations and places. Every true believer senses that unity with true believers in groups other than his own.

Yet another unity must have been prayed for. It is obvious that the purpose of this unity was to be a testimony to the world. If it is to be such a testimony, it must be a visible unity. All the sectarianism and fragmentization of the Church is therefore a violation of this prayer and is an obstacle to its answer today. One of the great sins of our modern era is the sin of schism and we must be courageous enough to face it. There is a necessity for examining our practices and beliefs to ascertain whether we are sinning against the will and prayer of Christ or not.

II. Christian Striving for Unity

The invitation of Romanism to Protestant branches of Christendom to return to the mother church is often repeated, but it is based upon the bigoted claim that the Roman Catholic Church is the only church, that all other branches are false and that it is necessary for us to repent and to return to Roman Catholicism. In this invitation there is an absence of repentance for the historic evils of the Church, an absence of reformation of life of the Church and a failure to return to the New Testament doctrines and life. Romanism has departed so far from primitive Christianity as exemplified in the Bible that it is guilty of schism in separating itself from all believers who attempt to reproduce that primitive Christian life. A large proportion of the guilt of causing division in the church, with the resulting schism, rests upon the shoulders of the Roman Church itself and we may anticipate for this truly wicked organization the fulfillment of the prophecy of Revelation 17. The Roman Church is certainly identified with "the great whore that sitteth upon many waters." In spite of all our abhorrence of schism, of division and of fragmentization of the Church, we could never advance the unity of the Church by returning to Rome. Rome has departed from New Testament Christianity.

The impossibility of Protestant union is just as apparent. There is a new breath of unity in the Protestant church in these days, expressed in a desire for amalgamation of denominations, in the formation of a National Church, and ultimately of a World Church. Steps are being taken toward this end everywhere. Hardly a month goes by but we hear of the approaches of one denomination to another for the purpose of unity; and sometimes they are denominations far separated from one another in ecclesiology and in doctrine. Dr. E. Stanley Jones even goes so far as to advocate a National American Church with various branches, including the Roman Catholic Church as one branch. This is the mood of our day.

The non-orthodox elements are so prominent in the union movement of Protestantism that Biblical Christians find it very difficult to take any part in the union movement. These cooperative interchurch movements are largely modernistic and liberal and in some cases even Unitarian. The importance of conviction and doctrine is pared down in the interests of unity and cooperation. Such unity can never be effective.

It was for this reason that a large group of evangelical leaders organized the National Association of Evangelicals as an attempt on the part of evangelical, Bible-believing Christians to associate in communion. In 1943, after a year of preliminary existence as a temporary organization the movement was crystallized in a great constitutional convention in Chicago with the adoption of a statement of faith, a constitution and a policy of action. Already seventeen denominations are associated with the National Association of Evangelicals and many individual evangelical churches have united with the movement. Its constituents number over a million. Already the National Association of Evangelicals has become the united voice of orthodox Protestantism with commissions working in eight inter-denominational fields of endeavor. Already it is achieving the cooperation of most evangelical, interdenomination movements within the framework of its organization. Many of these interdenominational movements have affiliated as subsidiaries of the National Association of Evangelicals. The genius of the National Association of Evangelicals, however, is not divisive. It does not require withdrawal from the historic denominations. No denomination can unite with the National Association of Evangelicals if it belongs to a similar interdenominational movement; but individual churches within the framework of denominations that belong to other interdenominational movements may repudiate their allegiance to that interdenominational representative and designate the National Association of Evangelicals as their voice for orthodoxy. It is not the desire of the leaders of the National Association of Evangelicals or of the movement further to fragmentize Christian groups, but rather to draw together evangelical believers of all denominations and organizations in an orthodox movement which will transcend these lines.

The inevitable trend of our day calls for a new alignment. Denominational lines in many cases are no longer important. They are often drawn on outworn controversies of former years and many of the adherents of these denominations do not know the particular emphasis of their denominations. The day has come when Bible believers in all denominations belong together and must come together under the banner of the cross or they must be left behind. This statement of faith of the National Association of Evangelicals of which we have been giving an exposition is the least basis of cooperation. It may be called the least common denominator of evangelical Christians. We recognize that many of the denominations and churches in the National Association of Evangelicals movement have gone beyond this in their own creeds, but they accept this in common with other denominations. Therefore, they can cooperate on an evangelical basis.

Today we evangelicals face organized government atheism, the possibility of social revolution and the antagonism of world secularism which surely will engulf the believer if he attempts to stand alone. We must be together with Christ and with each other. Therefore, let the Church be the Church — the holy, universal, apostolic Church.

III. CHRIST AND HIS CHURCH

Christ prayed for His Church, for the redeemed, and our text says that He loved the Church and gave Himself for it. He died to redeem for Himself a bride, a corporate body of believers, an organism. The blood of Calvary guaranteed the existence of such a body. Christ did not die in vain. God gave Him a people.

But Christ also loved me and gave Himself for me.

Only by my realization of what that Cross and blood did for me and an acceptance of it do I become a member of that Church or of the redeemed. Thus I am not alone. Christ died for me, but not for me only. I have many corporate responsibilities and my salvation reaches its expression in the Church — the body of the redeemed, God's redemptive agency on earth today. I cannot forget that as a believer I am a member of the Church.

Christ has given us a symbol of the unity of the redeemed. What is it that shows that I belong to Him and to other believers? It is the Lord's supper. At His table we meet with one another. There He is supreme and there we worship Him as one body of believers. We do not have and we never will have uniformity, but we can have unity in worship and in spirit and in the essence of our faith. No cathedral is made up of identical cubes or rhomboids. Each stone is cut to fit in a particular arch or pillar or wall. No two stones are alike. But when assembled the cathedral reveals the beauty of unity in diversity and thus it is with the Church. Union will come by communion. We must have a communion of belief, of love, of fellowship and of worship. Let us go back to the primitive church where the disciples gathered for the breaking of bread and fellowship and continued in the apostles' doctrine and in prayer. Christ was there in their midst and He may be in the midst of the Church today.

The figures of our unity as the redeemed are many. We might use the figure of an army. In an effective, conquering army, all are not generals; all do not belong to the artillery; all do not belong to the infantry; all are not aviators and all are not motorized units. All the individual units play a part in the larger picture and hence become an army — an efficient unit in obtaining victory. In the army are the motorized units, the infantry, the artillery, the intelligence corps. This is a figure of the kind of unity which we must have in the Church. Let the Church march as a glorious army under the banner of Christ and His generalship.

This leads us to a second figure, that of a symphony orchestra. As one sits waiting for the conductor to enter he often hears many individual players, each playing his own piece upon his instrument. There are the oboe and the trumpet and the violin and the bass viol and the cymbals. The total sound is a jumble of noise. Each one may be playing a very pretty piece if it were played alone in a home or as a solo, but when played with two or three score other pieces that do not harmonize it is a crashing din. Soon, however, the conductor enters and those instrumental players who see him first cease their activity. Usually most of the players will have become silent by the time he mounts the rostrum. Sometimes it is necessary for him to tap his baton in order to silence the last player. Then with every eye upon him, he lifts his arms and in a moment of time the glorious harmony of the symphony begins. That is what we must do. We must get our eyes upon Christ. We must be watching Him. We must not be playing our own little pieces, going our own way, but under His direction, guidance and leadership, we must form the symphony of harmony in the unity of the Church.

Another figure, a Biblical figure, is His body. Every part has a functional interest and only as it performs that functional purpose will it accomplish its destiny and participate in the unity of the whole. There is an intercommunication of faith and life in the parts of the body and this there must be in the Church. Christ Himself is the head and source of all.

Christ is calling such a Church to witness for His Name. The Church is not to be identical with the world. We have no promise that the Church will convert the world. Therefore, let the Church be the Church. Then when it reaches its fullness, as it some day will, He will take it unto Himself, a glorious Church without spot or wrinkle or any such thing, for its destiny will have been reached and its purpose fulfilled. That Church washed in His blood should include you and me. "We believe in the spiritual unity of believers in Christ."

www.ingramcontent.com/pod-product-compliance
Lightning Source LLC
LaVergne TN
LVHW021620080426
835510LV00019B/2681